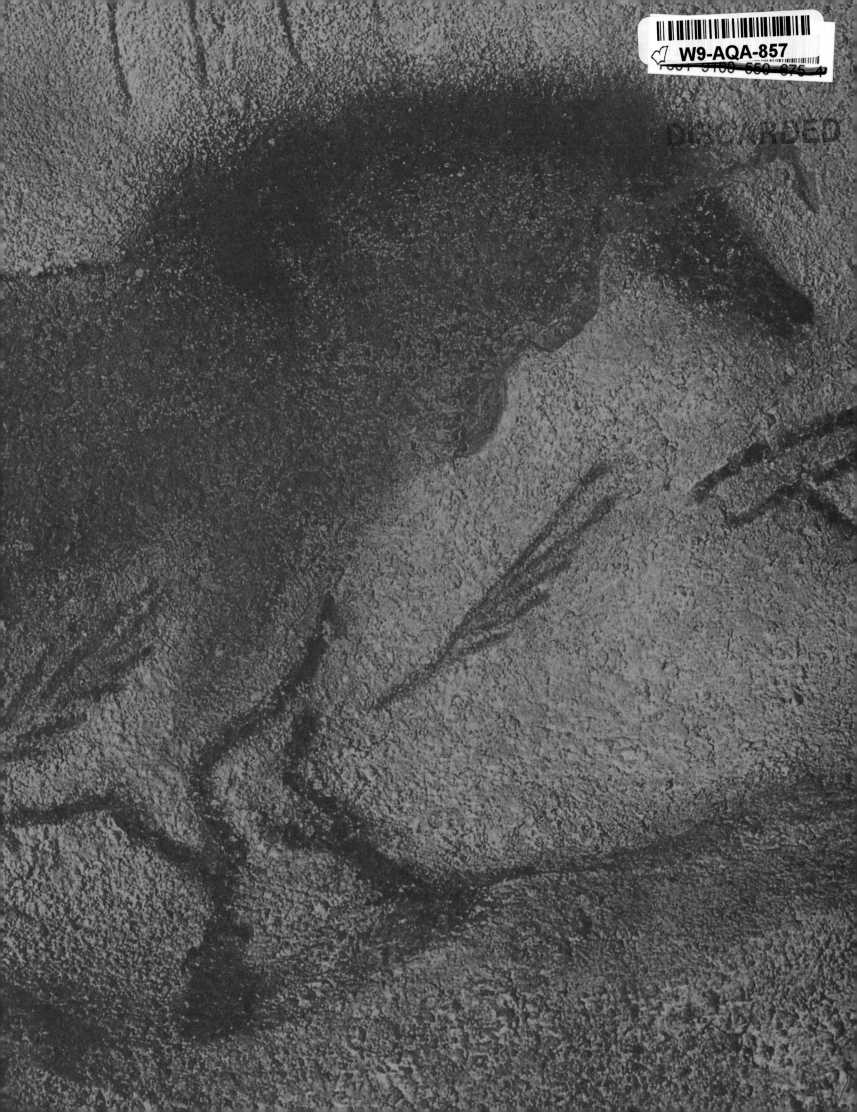

THE STORY OF

PAINTINGS

A History of Art for Children

by Mick Manning and
Brita Granström

STERLING CHILDREN'S BOOKS
New York

Contents

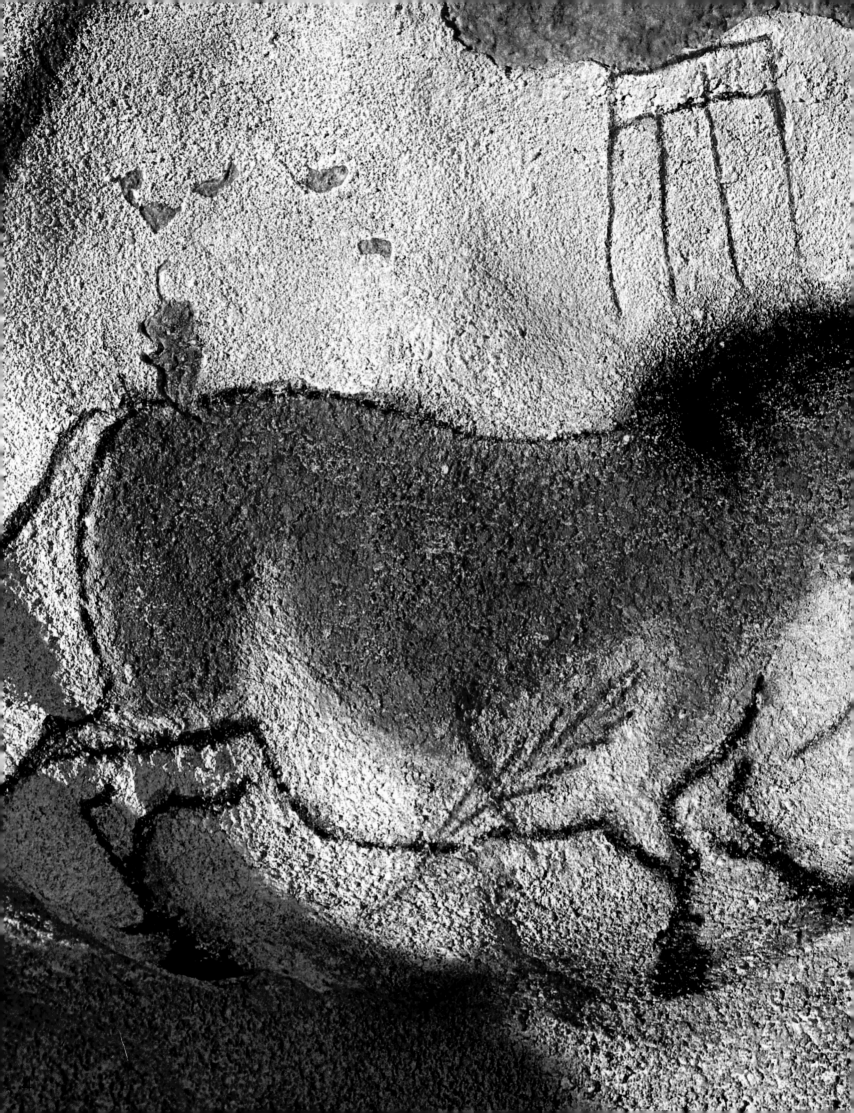

Lascaux Cave Paintings

by a Stone Age Artist, c. 15,500 BCE

Painting began as a sort of magic thousands of years ago! During the Stone Age, humans spent most of their time finding food and staying warm to keep alive—and yet they still made paintings on cave walls. In the dark, secret Lascaux cave, this painting of a galloping wild horse, made about 17,500 years ago, would have seemed to come to life when viewed in flickering firelight. Perhaps such paintings were a backdrop for ceremonies long forgotten? Perhaps Stone Age people believed their artists possessed magic powers?

The oldest European cave art dates back nearly 50,000 years. Known cave painting sites include Lascaux, Chauvet Cave, and Font-de-Gaume in France and Creswell Crags in England.

Our paintings help make these caves sacred spaces. We paint the animals we hunt for our food.

We use red clays, colored rocks, berries, and charcoal to paint our pictures.

Our Story Begins

So painting began as a sort of magic first exhibited in dark caves! We've presented this book as a sort of art exhibition, too—one that time-travels across centuries from the Stone Age to the 20th century. The story of painting is awe-inspiring and, because we could only exhibit 39 paintings in our book, it would have been impossible to choose which ones without a few guidelines. So, to tell our story, we decided to focus on paintings *we* loved and show them in the order they were painted; many are famous paintings, mixed with some others you might not have seen before. Finally, we decided not to show living artists but those who have now passed into art history themselves.

So get ready to feast your eyes on our exhibition of great art.

Ancient Civilizations

Painting developed as ancient civilizations used pictures for both religious reasons and to decorate objects. Artists ground up their own pigment powders from rocks, lead, and minerals, but later began to mix in egg yolk (tempera) or oil (oil paint) to make it gooey. It wasn't until the middle of the 19th century that people began to manufacture ready-mixed paints.

Egyptian tomb wall paintings show us their gods and goddesses. This one, made around 1279–1213 BCE, depicts the god Anubis finishing the mummification of a pharaoh.

The gods and goddesses on the walls will help people buried here to travel to the afterlife.

6

The ancient Greeks, from the early Minoan period to the Classical era (c. 3500–300 BCE), painted frescoes on the walls of important houses and palaces both to decorate them and make them feel like special and powerful places.

Our art makes people look bigger and braver, like heroes and gods.

The Romans evolved the Classical Greek style to be more realistic. This beautiful and lifelike coffin portrait was one of many made by artists in Egypt when it was ruled by the Romans.

My coffin paintings make the people inside live forever!

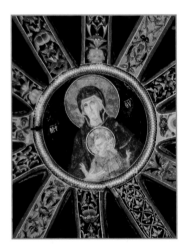

By the 4th century CE, more and more people in Europe and around the Eastern Mediterranean were becoming Christian. Byzantine artists celebrated Christian teaching and Bible stories by decorating the walls and ceilings of magnificent churches.

We paint to strict styles and try to make our art timeless.

By the 14th century artists were becoming more important and often famous. It was a time we call the Early Renaissance when European artists, writers, and scientists began to think about the world in new and exciting ways at the same time as rediscovering the great art of the Romans and the Greeks. Painters learnt their craft from "masters," working as apprentices until they were well-known enough to set up their own studios.

Let's look at what happened next over the centuries in more detail.

At this time, the Catholic Church paid artists to illustrate Biblical events on church walls.
Not everyone could read then, so these images helped to teach Bible stories.

The Lamentation

by Giotto di Bondone, c. 1266/7–1337

Some say that Italian artist Giotto was a shepherd boy, others that he was a blacksmith's son. We can't be sure either is true. However we are sure that Giotto's masterworks are the frescoes (wall paintings) of the Scrovegni Chapel in Padua. Completed around 1305, these tell the lives of Jesus Christ and the Virgin Mary, his mother. *The Lamentation* shows Mary grieving (or lamenting) over her son's body after the crucifixion, when Jesus was put to death. Giotto used everyday people as models for Biblical characters. He shows their great sadness—look at their expressions and the child-like faces of the angels.

The story goes that young Giotto was taken on as an apprentice by the great Florentine painter Cimabue.

One day, as a joke, Giotto painted a fly on one of his master's paintings.

It was so realistic that Cimabue tried several times to brush it off.

The Arnolfini Portrait

by Jan van Eyck, 1390–1441

Dutchman Jan van Eyck was a master painter running his own studio by 1422. By now, paintings were not just found in churches and palaces but in the homes of wealthy people. *The Arnolfini Portrait*, painted in 1434, was commissioned by van Eyck's friend, rich Italian merchant Giovanni di Nicolao Arnolfini. It shows him posing alongside his wife at their home in the Flemish city of Bruges. What clues can you spot that suggest the Arnolfinis' wealth?

Look at the tiny details:

 *the individual highlights on the orange and other fruit by the window;*

 *the faithful little dog, a symbol of loyalty;*

in the little mirror, you can see the artist himself, with another unknown figure.

This painting, with its thin layers of oil paint creating the soft daylight filtering into the dark interior, is one of the most influential and touching portraits in the history of Western art.

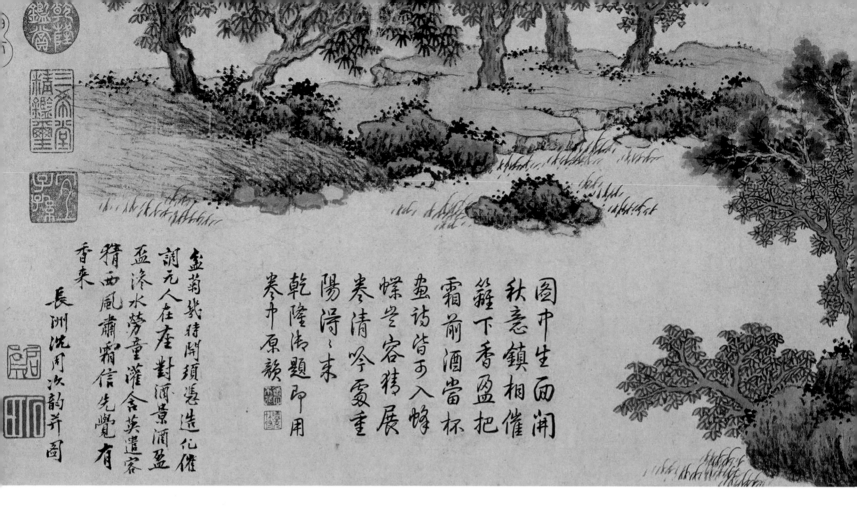

Appreciating Potted Chrysanthemum in Tranquility

by Shen Zhou, 1427–1509

I feel at peace as I write and paint.

China's long tradition of art developed completely separately from that in Europe. Shen Zhou was a Chinese painter working during the famous Ming Dynasty (1368–1664). He upheld the ancient Chinese tradition of combining the "Three Perfections" in his work—painting, poetry, and calligraphy (beautiful handwriting). From a wealthy background, Shen Zhou lived a reclusive life, devoting his time to artwork, and contemplating nature and life with his many artistic friends. His art shows a master's confidence in bold lines and shapes but also a calmness and warmth. His style makes the most of the moist and flowing qualities of brush and ink.

The poem, written out in Shen Zhou's exquisite calligraphy, captures the moment he depicts in the painting. A group of friends meet to discuss and appreciate the potting of flowers in a tranquil garden surrounded by nature's beauty. What could be more peaceful than this?

Shen Zhou's love of nature began a new tradition of painting flowers and birds in Chinese art. Look at **Turtledove Calling for Rain** or the lilies he painted in his **Album of Sketching from Life**.

When I finish a painting, it takes on a life of its own.

The Hunt in the Forest

by Paolo Uccello, 1397–1475

Italian Paolo Uccello was apprenticed to a sculptor at about the age of ten and by 1424 was earning his own living as a painter, traveling to Venice, Rome, and Bologna. Uccello was excited by the new mathematical ideas of perspective and used them to create a feeling of depth in his paintings.

The Hunt in the Forest is Uccello's last known painting, made around 1470. It shows his breathtaking mastery of perspective. Notice how the hunters, horses, and dogs lead your eye deeper and deeper into the mysterious forest and how the colors and tones change the farther away you look.

What a fascinating thing this perspective is!

Using ideas of perspective, Uccello explored with mathematical accuracy how the size and angles of things changed depending on your viewpoint.

On one of his famous paintings *Saint George and the Dragon,* he painted chessboard style grass to give the illusion of space.

Other Uccello paintings to look at: **Saint George and the Dragon** and **The Battle of San Romano**. And look at the work of Piero della Francesca (c. 1415–1492) for another master of perspective.

Look at some other beautiful Botticelli paintings featuring gods and goddesses: **Primavera** (also known as **Allegory of Spring**) and **Venus and Mars**.

Aaagh! How shocking!

Some of Botticelli's paintings were considered "un-Christian" by the all-powerful Catholic Church.

The Birth of Venus

by Sandro Botticelli, c. 1445–1510

Sandro began as an apprentice for the famous artist Fra Filippo Lippi who taught him how to paint people, faces, and skin with great skill. Each person is unique and beautiful. His most famous work, *The Birth of Venus* (mid-1480s), shows us Venus, the pagan goddess of love and beauty, blown to shore in a seashell by a wind god and goddess (left). Venus looks out of the painting at us as she waits for a goddess of summer (right) to wrap her in a cloak of flowers.

The model for Venus is thought to be Simonetta Cattaneo Vespucci, a great beauty and favorite of the Medici court in Florence. It is possible that Botticelli may have painted himself as the wind god.

Most of my fellow painters are still inspired by the Bible, but in my pictures I like to celebrate Roman pagan myths about love and the seasons.

Mona Lisa

by Leonardo da Vinci, 1452–1519

Da Vinci was one of the greatest artists of the Italian Renaissance—as well as an inventor, mathematician, and all around genius. *Mona Lisa* (1503–19) is his most famous painting; people are captivated by her sideways glance and gentle smile. What do you think she's smiling about?

Like other Renaissance artists, Leonardo was interested in perspective and used mathematical devices and grids to make his paintings. Can you see how he is using the grid method to view his model?

Some other paintings by Leonardo da Vinci to look at: **The Last Supper, The Virgin of the Rocks, Lady with an Ermine,** *and* **St. John the Baptist**.

19

The Sistine Chapel Ceiling

by Michelangelo, 1475–1564

Michelangelo was known as a sculptor as much as a painter but, from the age of 13, he had learnt his trade from Domenico Ghirlandaio, a fresco painting master. So, in 1508, when he was asked to paint some frescoes on the ceiling supports of the Vatican's Sistine Chapel, Michelangelo persuaded the Pope to let him tackle the entire 5,000-square-foot ceiling instead, not to mention a wall as well! It took him four years to finish this masterpiece and it is now visited by around six million tourists a year, who stand in line to gaze in wonder at over 300 heavenly figures "floating" above their heads.

To paint directly on the chapel's 66-foot-high ceiling, Michelangelo used his own design of wooden scaffolding platforms so he and his plasterers could reach.

Can you spot some famous Biblical scenes?

The great danger lies not in setting our aim too high and falling short, but setting our aim too low, and achieving our mark . . .

Go on, Eve. Try this tasty apple!

And I, God, create Man.

The Ambassadors

by Hans Holbein the Younger, c. 1497–1543

Hans Holbein was German but became court painter to Henry VIII, the powerful king of England, infamous for chopping off the heads of two of his six wives. *The Ambassadors* shows two important Frenchmen who visited court in 1533; it is full of mysterious symbols and clues. For example, the ages of the sitters are recorded on the dagger's sheath and on the book on the top shelf, while various scientific instruments give the date and time the painting was made: April 11 at 10.30 a.m. Can you work out what that shape at the front of the painting is meant to be? Viewed from the correct angle, you will see it is a human skull! Perhaps it was to remind people death may be just around the corner and to lead a good life.

This painting style is known as "anamorphic" and means a painting distorted to create an illusion. Holbein was in the business of creating illusions: his spectacular pictures made the people they featured look rich, strong, and, in Henry's case, an all-powerful king.

Make me look bigger and stronger!

Look at Holbein's portraits of Henry VIII, Thomas Cromwell, and Sir Thomas More.

24

Hunters in the Snow

by Pieter Bruegel the Elder, c. 1525–1569

Bruegel was a Dutch Renaissance painter best known for his paintings of ordinary people. In Bruegel's time most painters painted rich people or religious scenes. In this winter scene (1565), three hunters are returning home accompanied by a rag-tag pack of dogs. As they crest the hill a huge snowy panorama opens out. It's a feast for our eyes, filled with amazing details; a time capsule, showing us what life was like on a winter's day in the 1500s.

We call him "Peasant Bruegel" because some say he dresses up like a poor peasant and blends in with the crowds.

He gains inspiration for his paintings from everyday people and life.

Other paintings by Bruegel to look at: **The Peasant Wedding, The Blind Leading the Blind, Landscape with the Fall of Icarus,** *and* **Children's Games**.

Vegetables in a Bowl or The Gardener

by Giuseppe Arcimboldo, 1527–1593

Giuseppe Arcimboldo was born in Milan, Italy but became a painter of portraits to the Hapsburg court in Vienna and later to the court in Prague. His most famous portraits appear normal at a distance, but the closer you look the stranger they get, because they are made up from vegetables, plants, fruits, sea creatures, and tree roots! He liked visual jokes such as the "topsy-turvy" painting opposite called *Vegetables in a Bowl* or *The Gardener*. Try turning the book upside down to see why! Which way up do you think is right?

Look at Arcimboldo's set of four paintings **The Four Seasons** which express all the character of the different seasons in four haunting faces made up of seasonal fruits, vegetables, and plants.

Some people think I am crazy! But they have no sense of humor. My paintings are meant to be fun.

The Card Sharps

by Michelangelo Merisi da Caravaggio, 1571–1610

Italian artist Caravaggio was a master painter and a master storyteller. Here an expensively dressed boy is playing cards, but we can see what he can't—he is being tricked! The second boy is cheating with extra cards behind his back while the older man with the tatty gloves, his partner in crime, signals to him what cards the foolish boy is holding. The dagger at the cheat's side shows that violence may be a last resort to steal the fool's money. Look at the clever use of light and shade to light up the scene—in the same way studio photographers try to make portraits today.

Caravaggio created this painting when he had just set up on his own after years of finishing details on his master's paintings as an apprentice. It was so popular he may have painted several versions.

Look at some more of Caravaggio's studio paintings: **The Supper at Emmaus**, *a religious painting, and the three different versions of* **The Lute Player**.

I lead a wild life—but painting always comes first.

Self-Portrait as a Young Man

by Rembrandt van Rijn, 1606–1669

Dutch painter Rembrandt was famous for his portraits. As a young man, his paintings became fashionable and were bought by rich clients including the Dutch royal court. As well as painting other people, Rembrandt was also fascinated by painting himself and, over his career, painted many striking self-portraits. This one was painted around 1628, when he was only 22. Like Caravaggio before him, Rembrandt was a master of chiaroscuro—the dramatic use of light and shade. Here the light falls boldly over his face but, although his eyes are in shadow, they stare intently out at us. Rembrandt also liked to play with the texture of the paint—in this picture, he used the wooden end of his paint brush to show the curls in his hair.

Take a look at other self-portraits by Rembrandt, painted at different times in his life. How does his use of paint vary? And why do you think he was so interested in painting his own portrait?

Life etches itself out on our faces as we grow older . . .

Rembrandt was paid very well for his work and by 1639 he and his wife Saskia could afford to move to a newly built house in Amsterdam (now the Rembrandt House Museum).

But Rembrandt spent his money too easily and fell into debt. He was forced to sell his lovely house and this great artist died a poor man, buried in an unknown grave.

The Maids of Honor

by Diego Velázquez, 1599–1660

Often known by its Spanish name, *Las Meninas,* this painting's clever composition presents a puzzle. Painted in 1656 at the royal court of Spain, it shows the young princess Margaret Theresa and her maids of honor. But why is the Royal Chamberlain, an important man, waiting in the doorway and why is the painter, Velázquez, in the picture? And why is everyone looking at us? It is a fascinating group portrait that has kept people guessing for centuries. Look in the mirror. Is the answer there? Reflected in it are King Philip IV of Spain and his queen. Is Velázquez allowing us to feel like royalty posing for our portrait?

Here are some things to find:

Pick out the king and queen in the mirror. Does it remind you of another picture (see page 11)?

I live and work in the royal court, so I know the royal family well.

I'm a precious princess—the heir to the Spanish throne.

How does the princess stand out from her maids?

Hey. I'm trying to sleep!

Could it be a bit boring watching a portrait be painted?

The Love Letter

by Johannes Vermeer, 1632–1675

By the 17th century, the subjects people painted were much more varied. Dutch artist Vermeer specialized in homely scenes of middle-class life set inside the same two small rooms at his own house in Delft. In this painting, Vermeer shows us a very private moment—a maid who has interrupted her chores (notice the mop and the dirty laundry) to deliver a love letter to her surprised looking mistress. Vermeer often uses a view through a door to make us feel we are witnessing private events.

Look at the details: the wall hanging, the folded curtain. Enjoy Vermeer's clever use of the checkered floor pattern to give a feeling of depth (remember Uccello on page 14) and the lovely feeling of light flooding into the room.

What details can you spot?

Can you find the love letter?

The maid's mop?

I love how the light catches her earring.

Whose are these shoes?

Other Vermeer paintings to look at: **The Art of Painting, Girl with the Pearl Earring,** *and* **A Young Woman Standing at a Virginal***.*

Still Life of Flowers on a Table Ledge

by Rachel Ruysch, 1664–1750

In Rachel Ruysch's day women found it difficult to have the independence to become professional artists. However Rachel Ruysch succeeded and became one of Holland's most famous painters, specializing in a genre we call still life. Rachel became the apprentice of Willem van Aelst, a well-known Amsterdam painter, and by the time she was eighteen she was selling her own paintings. Despite having ten children during her life, she continued her successful career that spanned over 60 years. Her paintings, such as *Still Life of Flowers on a Table Ledge* (1700), show strongly detailed compositions that use rich, brilliant colors and flowing natural lines, a style that is part of the movement we know as Rococo. It may be a flower arrangement—but look at the insects, small and large, lurking among the plants.

Rachel's father was a scientist with a vast collection of natural history specimens that Rachel drew from an early age.

Still life, which depicts unmoving objects, is an art genre that still exists today in many styles, but it was made famous by realistic Dutch painters during the 17th and 18th centuries.

Look at the fantastic stylized curving shapes of elephant and tiger locked in combat. Notice the blood on the poor elephant's legs and trunk from the tiger's teeth and claws.

Some other pictures by Mir Kalan Khan (or attributed to him) have much more elaborate backgrounds. Look at **Lovers in a Landscape** and **A Vision of an Elephant Hunt**.

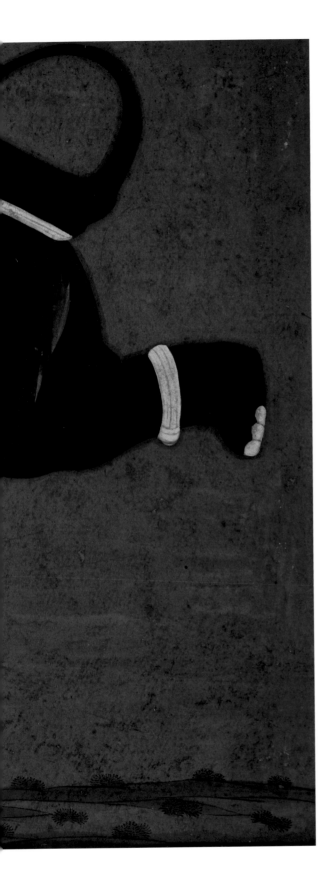

Mughal painters in India developed an interest in animals and plants painted realistically.

An Elephant and Rider Trampling a Tiger

by Mir Kalan Khan, active c. 1760–1780

Artists are always influenced by other artists. By the mid-18th century, Western painters were becoming more aware of Asian art—and Asian artists were picking up Western ideas. India at the time was ruled by the Mughal emperors, but they were coming increasingly under the influence of European countries, who were trading and setting up colonies there. Many beautiful paintings were made in the Indo-Islamic courts of Lucknow and Hyderabad, often for the Europeans living there. These include this romantic painting of a tiger hunt painted by the acclaimed artist Mir Kalan Khan of Lucknow.

Catfight

by Francisco Goya, 1746–1828

Perhaps this painting isn't just about cats—perhaps Goya is making a statement about people and their battles. Do our leaders behave no better than fighting tomcats?

Spanish artist Francisco José de Goya is seen by many as a bridge between the style of the Old Masters of the previous centuries and the more Romantic ideas about art that emerged in the 19th century. He became rich as a formal court painter, but his more personal art picked up on the changing mood of the time, expressing strong emotions and political views. *Catfight* (1786) was commissioned to hang over the door of a well-to-do dining room. Look at the aggression and anger as two tomcats, fur upright, face each other before a fight. We can almost imagine the yowls they are making.

*Compare the style of this picture with his **The Third of May, 1808** and his portrait of **The Duke of Wellington** (the general who led the British against the French in the Peninsular War).*

In 1808, France attacked Spain in the Peninsular War. This terrible war and the deaths it brought inspired Goya to make many anti-war paintings and prints including his famous The Third of May, 1808.

Martin became firm friends with his lively teacher, Bonifacio Musso. Musso had not only eloped to England with a novice nun but taught fencing as well as art.

For a while in London Martin shared lodgings and worked for Bonifacio's son, Charles Muss. Muss was a successful painter too but never achieved Martin's fame.

The Destruction of Pompeii and Herculaneum

by John Martin, 1789–1854

British artist John Martin was born in the wild country in Northumberland, close to Hadrian's Wall. As a young man he moved to Newcastle, where he was taught by the Italian artist Bonifacio Musso. Later he moved to London. John's large, dramatically-lit, panoramic landscapes on Biblical and legendary themes captured the popular fashion for wild Romanticism. Here he imagines the famous volcanic eruption of Pompeii as it shoots out a molten cloud of red-hot ash and gushing rivers of lava. Look at the way the poisonous cloud curls above the ant-like humans.

Audiences would visit galleries to view Martin's paintings just as today people go to the cinema. In fact have you seen Peter Jackson's award-winning film of The Lord of The Rings? *It may remind you of this painting . . .*

Martin's art was often dismissed as too dramatic by the critics but the public loved it. Look at **The Great Day of His Wrath** *and* **Manfred and the Alpine Witch** *to see why.*

My paintings are bought by influential people—politicians and royalty!

To make a woodblock print, the artist draws a design on the wood and carves it out, so that the image stands out.

He rolls printing ink (a sort of sticky paint) onto the carved image. He prints this onto paper.

The Great Wave

by Katsushika Hokusai, 1760–1849

Hokusai was a Japanese artist born in Edo (now Tokyo). He was a printmaker rather than a painter, working in the East Asian traditions developed in China (see page 12) and Japan. However, his prints became popular in Europe and, without the influence of this Japanese art form, there might have been no Impressionism. Monet (see page 54) was a huge admirer of Hokusai's work.

The Great Wave is the first in Hokusai's best-known woodblock print series *Thirty-six Views of Mount Fuji* (c. 1831). Mount Fuji is an active volcano and the highest mountain in Japan. Hokusai's huge wave dwarfs it and the fishing boats. The wave seems to be a living thing with claws reaching to grasp the fishermen. Hokusai makes us think of the power of nature, found in water, wind, and fire.

I call myself "Old Man Mad About Art."

He lifts off the paper to reveal the print. Once it is dry, he adds other colors using different carved blocks.

Turner's father proudly began selling his 11-year-old son's paintings from his barber's shop. By 15, Turner was exhibiting at the famous Royal Academy Summer Exhibition.

He once added a red buoy to a painting when it was hanging on the wall of the Royal Academy. It completed the painting and astonished his fellow artists.

The Fighting Temeraire

by J.M.W. Turner, 1775–1851

British artist Joseph Mallard William Turner developed new ways of painting, using color and brushstrokes to capture the ever-changing weather. *The Fighting Temeraire,* painted in 1839, shows us an old ship, famous for taking part in the Battle of Trafalgar (1805), being towed away by a steam-powered tug boat to be scrapped. Turner paints it before a romantic sunset encouraging us to feel a patriotic sympathy for the old ship. She seems like a ghost. Turner suggests the glory days of the age of sail giving way to the new age of steam. It makes us think about the idea of the modern replacing the old—and youth and old age as well.

Look at some other Turner paintings: **The Slave Ship** *and* **Rain, Steam and Speed— The Great Western Railway**. *Turner also influenced the Impressionists—* *see page 54.*

Turner loved the sea and ships. It is said that he once tied himself to a ship's mast so he could experience a storm at sea without being washed overboard!

The sun is God.

The Starry Night

by Vincent van Gogh, 1853–1890

Dutch artist Vincent van Gogh only became a full-time painter in his late twenties but died tragically at the age of 37. He was a Post-Impressionist artist, inspired by the Impressionists (see page 54) but pushed their ideas further, using strong brushstrokes and simple shapes. Van Gogh was always troubled and anxious. Once, he cut off his ear and, for a while, was sent to a psychiatric hospital. Here he carried on painting and, in June 1889, made *The Starry Night,* a swirling night-time sky full of wonder and mystery. The bold color and spiraling shapes make the moon shine and the stars twinkle.

It is a kind of painting that changes in character and takes on a richness the longer you look at it.

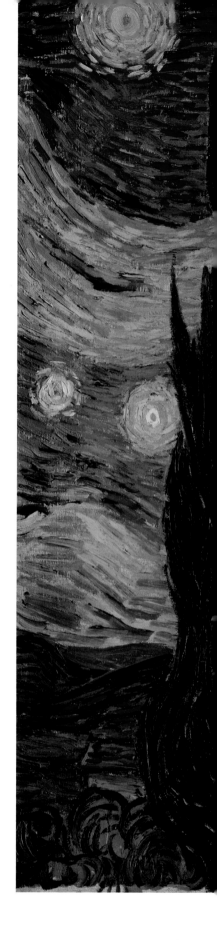

Van Gogh, sadly, shot himself and later died, not long after he painted one of his loneliest paintings, Wheat Field with Crows.

Van Gogh was not much admired when he was alive. Now people love his paintings such as **Sunflowers**, **Irises**, and **Wheat Field with Cypresses**.

In 1908, the great artist Pablo Picasso (see page 70) went to meet Rousseau after seeing a painting of his for sale on the street. He then held a banquet in Rousseau's honor. Some laughed at Rousseau, but his art influenced many modern artists, including Picasso, Chagall (page 62), and Salvador Dalí (page 66).

Tiger in a Tropical Storm or Surprised!

by Henri Rousseau, 1844–1910

Henri Rousseau was a self-taught painter and his childlike style is often called "primitive" or "naïve." You can see this in *Tiger in a Tropical Storm* (1891), a fantasy of a jungle in a monsoon. Look at the frightened tiger and the wild jungle shaken by the power of nature! Henri had never visited a real jungle, but he had visited the Paris Botanic Gardens and, of course, his imagination. Rousseau's art attracted younger artists moving away from the Impressionists, such as Henri Matisse (see page 60). In 1905, a Rousseau painting of a lion was hung alongside paintings by Matisse and other painters in a Paris exhibition that was criticized as the art of "wild beasts." Perhaps inspired by this and by Rousseau, many of these artists later formed the Fauves (French for "wild beasts"), a group of Post-Impressionist artists who worked with strong, brilliant colors.

Look at **The Hungry Lion Throws Itself on the Antelope,** *another jungle scene painted by Rousseau.*

Nothing makes me so happy as to observe nature and to paint what I see.

The Scream

by Edvard Munch, 1863–1944

As a boy, Norwegian artist Edvard Munch saw the illness and deaths of both his sister and mother, an experience he would never forget. Inspired amongst others by van Gogh (see page 48), he used color and shape to express in paint his own wild emotions about love, jealousy, loneliness, and loss. His masterwork *The Scream* (1893) put a haunting face to his own deep-felt anxieties with a use of vivid color (look at the blood-red sky) and simplified shapes (look at the boat pushed out from the headland in waves of energy). His haunting paintings were ahead of their time and inspired the birth of a new art movement in the early 20th century called Expressionism.

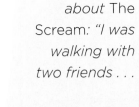

Munch wrote about The Scream: *"I was walking with two friends . . .*

"The sky became a bloody red . . . I felt a tinge of melancholy, stood there trembling with fright . . .

"I sensed an infinite scream passing through nature."

Hidden among the blood-red clouds I wrote in pencil: Could only have been painted by a madman!

In 1908, Munch was treated for a nervous breakdown in Denmark. He later returned to Norway and continued to paint.

Some other paintings by Munch to look at: **Self-Portrait. Between the Clock and the Bed** *(about old age),* **The Yellow Log** *(about death), and a beautiful portrait,* **Under the Chestnut Tree***.*

The Water-Lily Pond

by Claude Monet, 1840-1926

Like Turner, whose work he admired, Frenchman Claude Monet was fascinated by weather and light. He experimented with using paint in a new way that tried to capture how light and color constantly changed. In April 1874, Monet exhibited a painting called *Impression, Sunrise* that was to give his group of like-minded artists their name, the Impressionists. In 1883, Monet bought a country house and some adjoining water meadows. Here he made some magnificent lily ponds and began to paint them over and over again at different times of day, as the light changed.

In 1899 alone, Monet completed 12 paintings of the wooden bridge over one of his lily ponds. What time of day do you think this picture was painted?

As a young man, Monet sold charcoal cartoons for pocket money. He started using oil paint when he was 16.

The Impressionists believed in painting outdoors with oils straight onto the canvas. Monet even made himself a studio on a boat.

Monet lived to be over 80. He continued to paint his garden at Giverny.

Look at some paintings by Alfred Sisley and Pierre-Auguste Renoir, two other founders of the Impressionists.

Dance in Gopsmor

by Anders Zorn, 1860–1920

Zorn was a Swedish artist who captured the spirit of Swedish country life in his sensuous, impressionistic paintings. He loved to paint people at the country dances held during the Swedish festival of Midsummer. They were often held in decorated farm buildings, and the women wore their traditional dresses (each region had its own pattern). You can almost listen to this painting! Imagine the fiddle music and the stamp of feet on the wooden floorboards as these dancers, mostly poor rural farm workers, whirl and stomp with joy. The light and the blurry flashes of red ribbons give such a feel of movement to this noisy painting.

Zorn loved to paint women. He often used his own servants or other local girls as models.

Zorn became very wealthy. As well as a large house and studio, he owned a nearby cottage and a scatter of farm buildings he called Gopsmor. He went there to paint lakeside scenes with his models.

Like Bruegel, I love to paint country people.

Zorn was a globally successful artist. He painted the portraits of three U.S. presidents. He maintained his Swedish roots, and he and his wife, Emma, left their large art collection to the people of Sweden.

The Red-Checkered Tablecloth

by Pierre Bonnard, 1867–1947

Pierre Bonnard was a French painter known for his intense use of color to evoke bright light and shadow, both in his sunny interior and outdoor paintings. He usually painted people he knew, especially his beloved wife, Martha. He painted her at all times: dressed and undressed, from eating breakfast to lying in the bathtub. Here she is at the table. Its tablecloth's checkered pattern gives us that sense of perspective we have seen in Vermeer (see page 34). Look at the light highlights on Martha's blouse. Notice how Bonnard shows us how the light transforms the white paneling to blues. Then notice the black dog's head and how it works like a period, anchoring the painting and balancing Martha's graceful pose.

Bonnard made the paintings from memory backed up by his many drawings made from life and sometimes also using black-and-white photography—then still a very new idea.

Before I start painting I reflect, I dream.

Rather than using an easel, Bonnard liked to pin his canvases to a wall and work on several at once.

58

Goldfish

by Henri Matisse, 1869–1954

French artist Henri Matisse explored new ideas and ways of making art throughout his long career. He loved color and movement from the start, as you can see in his early Fauve (French for "wild beast") art. In this slightly later 1911 painting he uses color to focus our attention on the fish. Look at how the rich orange contrasts with the greens and other background colors.

When Matisse became too ill to paint and was bedbound, he experimented with colored paper, making bold cut paper shapes.

Matisse sometimes painted larger pictures using a brush attached to a bamboo pole to extend his reach.

An artist is an explorer.

I wouldn't mind turning into a vermillion goldfish.

Cutting into color reminds me of the sculptor's direct carving.

Some other paintings to look at by Matisse: **Portrait of Madame Matisse**, **Dance** *(there are lots of different versions),* **The Red Room**, *and* **The Snail** *(for his cut-outs). You might like to compare some of Matisse's work with Picasso's, too.*

The Birthday

by Marc Chagall, 1887–1985

Marc Chagall was born in Belarus, then part of Russia, and, despite prejudice against his Jewish background, he went to art school in Saint Petersburg before moving to Paris. Partly through homesickness he developed a dream-like style of painting based on memories of home and East European Jewish folk culture. His paintings show us people floating in an often amusing dream world and do delightful things to our imagination. In *The Birthday,* Chagall's beloved first wife, Bella, leans towards the window as Chagall himself floats above her and kisses her tenderly. It is a painting full of love and warmth.

Chagall once wrote about Bella that: "It is as if she knows everything about my childhood, my present, my future, as if she can see right through me."

Love and fantasy go hand in hand.

Autoportrait (Tamara in the Green Bugatti)

by Tamara de Lempicka, 1898–1980

Tamara de Lempicka came from an aristocratic Polish family and by the age of 17 had married and moved to live in Russia. During the Russian Revolution, she fled to Paris where she began to paint. By the 1920s Tamara was living a wild, bohemian life and glamour and fashion magazines celebrated her beauty and style as they would a modern TV celebrity. Her 1929 painting *Autoportrait (Tamara in the Green Bugatti)* shows us the liberated and independent woman she was and that other women dreamed they could become. Shockingly for the time, Tamara stares at us in a cool and confident way as she zooms by in a fashionable green Bugatti sports car.

I shall become a painter.

Tamara arrived in Paris with barely any money and sold her family jewels to live on. But then she began to paint . . .

Tamara made a big impression in Paris and Italy with her first exhibitions and became famous for both her paintings and wild lifestyle.

Do you like my car?

Tamara's portraits of herself and of others show the clean lines and shapes of the Art Deco style. They had great strength at a time when women were still struggling to be considered equal to men.

What do you think this picture is about? Is Dalí saying to us that
our lives are measured by the sound of the ticking of clocks?

The Persistence of Memory

by Salvador Dalí, 1904–1989

The Surrealist art movement explored the personal world of dreams and nightmares. One of its leaders, the Spaniard Salvador Dalí, developed a unique style that left behind the laws of nature. As a young man, Dalí grew long hair and his trademark long moustache. It made him one of the most recognized artists of the 20th century. *The Persistence of Memory* is an image of soft, melting pocket watches; one flops over a branch, another melts with a fly crawling on it, while ants cover the small orange clock, a symbol of decay. In the middle of the painting there is a face, a sort of self-portrait, wearing a soft clock like a saddle. Its huge eye is closed. Is it the exhausted dreamer of this dream?

Each morning when I awake, I experience again a supreme pleasure— that of being Salvador Dalí.

Summer Days

by Georgia O'Keeffe, 1887–1986

By the mid-1920s, Georgia O'Keeffe was one of America's most important artists. She was living in an exciting new age of jazz music and a design style known as Art Deco. Her luscious flower paintings echoed this spirit of the age and she became famous for these rhythmic, organic shapes. Between 1929 and 1949, she spent part of every year living in New Mexico where she would collect animal bones and rocks from the desert to feature in her paintings, such as the deer skull in *Summer Days* of 1936. She plays with her images and their scale against the desert mountain background to create an intense, dreamlike effect.

> I found I could say things with color and shapes that I couldn't say any other way—things I had no words for.

O'Keeffe loved the outdoors.

She went on several rafting adventures down the Colorado river with friends.

Georgia was inspired by the desert landscape and spent as much time as she could in an area of New Mexico known as Ghost Ranch.

Portrait of Dora Maar

by Pablo Picasso, 1881–1973

Picasso is for many the most revolutionary artist *ever!* Like Matisse (see
page 60), his work changed and developed throughout his life. Pioneering
Cubism at the start of the century, he became famous for showing
us objects and people in new ways, changing shapes and perspectives
to make us think about not only *what* we see, but *why* we see it. This is just
one of many, many experimental portraits he made. Look at the thick paint
and how he has combined both a profile and full face portrait so we "see" all
of her face, and the playful way he painted her eyes, ears, and nose.
How would you paint a "Picasso" face?

Is it a good likeness?

*Here are a few other
works by Picasso
to look out for: **The
Old Guitarist** (from
his Blue Period), **Les
Demoiselles d'Avignon**
(which kick-started the
Cubism movement),
and **Guernica** (famous
for its depiction of the
horror of war).*

*Dora Maar was a photographer
from Argentina. She was one
of Picasso's "muses"—inspiring
many of his paintings for about
ten years from the late 1930s.*

71

Take Off

by Dame Laura Knight, 1877–1970

Laura Knight, already a popular British painter, was made an official war artist at the outbreak of World War II (1939). *Take Off* (1943) is a group portrait of a British Royal Air Force bomber crew: the navigator checks his map, the wireless operator fiddles with his transmitter while the pilot and co-pilot begin their take-off procedure. Taking several months to complete, the picture captures the tension and uncertainty of a crew preparing to risk their lives on a bombing raid. In fact the navigator in the picture, Raymond Frankish Escreet, was killed on a later raid. Very upset, Laura sent his family a photograph of the painting.

Laura was sent to paint RAF personnel, farm girls, and factory workers.

As a woman in a male-dominated art world, Laura Knight's success was very important because it paved the way for other women artists.

Look at these other paintings by Dame Laura Knight: **Corporal Elspeth Henderson and Sergeant Helen Turner**, **Ruby Loftus Screwing a Breech Ring**, *and* **The Nuremberg Trial**.

After the war ended I visited Germany to paint the trials of the war criminals at Nuremberg.

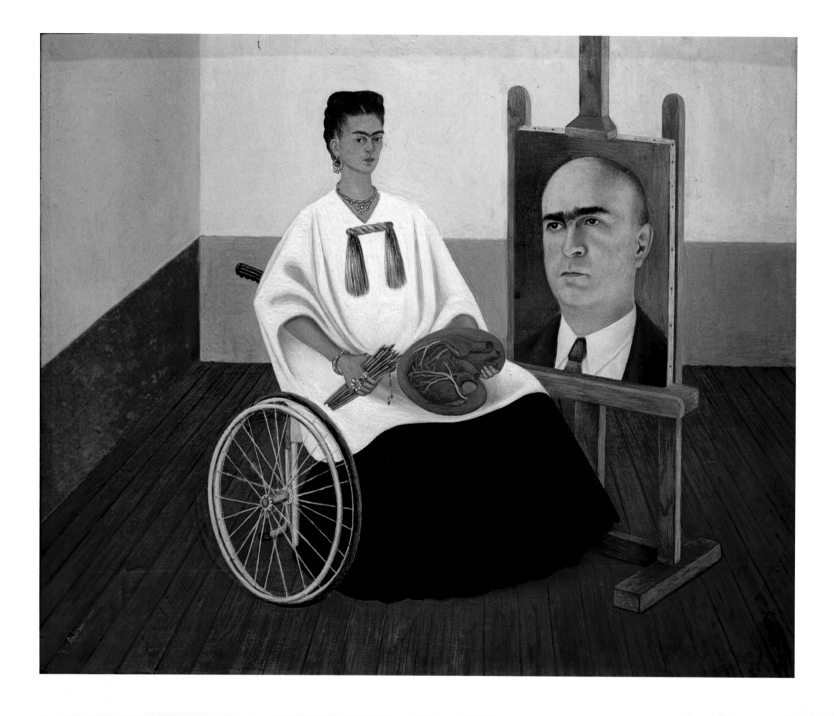

At only 18, Frida was badly injured in a bus accident.

She was in constant pain for the rest of her life and spent much of her time in a wheelchair.

Frida felt the accident was one of the most important moments in her life and often referred to it in her paintings.

Self-Portrait with Portrait of Doctor Farill

by Frida Kahlo, 1907–1954

Mexican artist Frida Kahlo developed a unique style of painting, heavily influenced by Mexican folk art. She often featured herself as a subject, partly to explore the pain she suffered for much of her life as a result of an accident. This late self-portrait was painted in November 1951. It features her surgeon, Dr Juan Farill, who had performed seven operations on her spine that year. Frida places his portrait as though it is an image of a saint, in recognition that he had saved her life. She works from a heart-shaped, blood-colored palette to show the strength of her feelings. Frida's use of strange symbols and images led her work to be compared with the Surrealists (see page 66), but she did not like this link, saying: "I never painted dreams. I painted my own reality."

She spent long periods of time in bed, which gave her plenty of time to think about her life and its meaning.

75

Blue Poles (Number 11, 1952)

by Jackson Pollock, 1912–1956

In the 20th century, many painters moved away from recognizable images and worked with color and shape in a way that did not represent objects, just ideas. In the USA this evolved into Abstract Expressionism. In 1936, Jackson Pollock began to experiment with liquid paint and painted with his canvases laid out on the studio floor. Pollock's style became known as "action painting." Critics often said that anyone could splatter paint like that, but Pollack's great color combinations and free shapes have depth and movement. Try it yourself and you'll see it isn't that easy.

Jackson called his style the "drip" technique and often used household paints with decorators' brushes and even sticks and syringes to squirt and splatter the paint about.

There are many other American Abstract Expressionists. Look at paintings by Mark Rothko, Lee Krasner, and Robert Richenburg for example.

On the floor, I am more at ease.

Fun Fair at Daisy Nook

by L.S. Lowry, 1887–1976

Although British artist Laurence Stephen Lowry went to the Manchester College of Art, he became a rent collector, retiring at 65, and only painted in his spare time. He developed his own distinctive style to capture the hustle, bustle, and hubbub of the factory workers, busy fairgrounds, and street scenes he loved so much. Just look at all the characters in *Fun Fair at Daisy Nook* (1953) and the good time they are having. Enjoy the feeling as your eye travels across the crowds and into the distance—does it remind you of the Bruegel painting on page 24? Lowry's paintings soon got noticed (and laughed at by some) for his "matchstick men" style, but those matchstick people make his paintings fizz with activity.

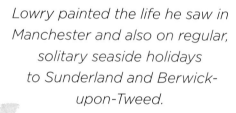

Lowry painted the life he saw in Manchester and also on regular, solitary seaside holidays to Sunderland and Berwick-upon-Tweed.

Take a look at Lowry's painting **Bridge St, Berwick-upon-Tweed**.

In the Car

by Roy Lichtenstein, 1923–1997

American Roy Lichtenstein studied art at the Ohio State University until his studies were interrupted by World War II. He served in the U.S. Army between 1943 and 1946 and then, after the war, became a teacher. By the 1960s he had developed a unique, enlarged comic-book style. Roy's love of teen-romance comics inspired many paintings such as *In the Car*. Look at the clever way Roy has simplified the color scheme to just a few colors and the "whizz lines" that both show reflections on the windows and make the car speed along. Roy's art reminds us all that graphic comic-book illustrations (often dismissed then as "commercial art") can be great art.

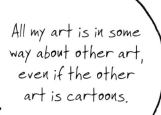

All my art is in some way about other art, even if the other art is cartoons.

Look at Lichtenstein's **Wham!**. *It shows a comic-book picture of a World War II fighter plane but greatly enlarged and recomposed.*

I love comics!

If you look close up at a vintage comic, you will notice the pictures are made up of colored "Ben-Day" dots. These dots vary in size and even overlap to make, light, shadow, and color.

Roy began to paint the dots by hand to create huge comic-style paintings.

Furious Man

by Jean-Michel Basquiat, 1960–1988

New Yorker Jean-Michel Basquiat adored his mother, but when he was 15 she was sent to a mental institution. After a troubled time, Jean-Michel dropped out of high school but luckily was sent to a school especially for artistic students, the City-As-School. After working with other street artists, Basquiat's solo career took off in the early 1980s. With his great talent and rock-star good looks, he got invited to fashionable parties in the New York art scene. His fresh, vibrant work explored poverty and racism using all the excitement of graffiti street art underpinned by great drawing. It began to sell for high prices—something Basquiat was uncomfortable with. He remained a rebel to the end.

Basquiat was a phenomenon. He died tragically of a drug overdose aged 27.

Do you think that is a halo or a crown above the man's head?

When Basquiat was eight years old, he was hit by a car and seriously injured.

The body is amazing.

While recovering, his favorite book was about anatomy. He was a clever boy and at 11 he could read and speak three languages: French, Spanish, and English.

From an early age his mother encouraged his talents and took him to art museums.

As a teenager Basquiat was a rebel, spraying his own graffiti art around New York.

83

Glossary

Abstract Expressionism: An influential American art movement that emerged after World War II that did not depict realistic objects but was led by color and shape.

ambassador: Someone who represents his country in another.

anamorphic: In art, describes an image that is distorted so it is seen differently from different viewpoints.

apprentice: A person who works for another in order to learn their trade or craft.

Art Deco: A decorative, angular art and design style from France, popular in the 1920s and 30s.

Bible, the: The book that holds the collected sacred writings of the Christian religion.

bohemian: Describes a wild and unusual lifestyle that breaks social rules.

Byzantine: The name given to the empire centred in Byzantium (modern Istanbul) that controlled land around the Mediterranean from the 4th to 15th centuries. Sometimes called the Eastern Roman Empire.

canvas: A cloth stretched on a frame to paint on, usually made of linen or cotton.

Catholic Church: The branch of Christianity led by the Pope in Rome. In early Renaissance times, most people in Western Europe were Catholic.

chiaroscuro: The use of strong light and shadow in a painting.

Christian: A follower of, or relating to, the religion based on the teachings of Jesus Christ.

Classical Greece: Refers to an important period in ancient Greek history from the 5th to 4th centuries BCE.

colony: A country or area of land where people from another country have settled, keeping links with their country of origin.

commercial art: Art created for the purposes of advertizing or selling.

court: In relation to royalty, the place where the royal family live and the people who live with them, making it a center of power.

Cubism: A revolutionary, early 20th-century style in painting where images were built up using geometric shapes and sometimes collage.

Expressionism: An early 20th-century art movement originating in Germany where artists tried to paint their emotions and moods.

Fauves: An early 20th-century group of French artists who used strong, contrasting color.

folk art: Art produced by people working in local traditions, which is often quite naïve in style.

genre: A style of art.

graffiti: Words or images written or painted on the walls of streets and other public places.

Hapsburg: The royal family that ruled Austria from the 13th to 20th centuries and the empire it controlled.

Impressionism: An art movement originating in France in the 1860s where artists tried to capture the impressions of the moment, especially of light and color.

jazz: A rhythmic and often wild style of music first popular in the 1920s.

Jewish: Describes the people who trace their roots back to the Hebrews of the Eastern Mediterranean who founded the religion of Judaism.

master: In art, a skilled artist who is in charge of his own studio.

merchant: Someone who makes a living by buying and selling goods.

Minoan: The early ancient Greek civilization focused on the island of Crete that lasted from about 3500 to 1000 BCE.

model: Someone who poses for an artist to draw or paint.

Mughal: A major ruling family of the Indian subcontinent from the 16th to 19th centuries.

Glossary

muse: A woman who inspires an artist, named after the ancient goddesses of arts and sciences said to inspire creative thoughts.

naïve: Childlike.

oil paint: A type of paint made from colored powder mixed with oil.

Old Master: A great artist from long ago, in particular one working in Europe between the 13th and the 17th centuries.

pagan: Not a Christian; usually of ancient religions that believed in many sorts of nature gods.

peasant: A farm laborer, particularly of the medieval era.

Peninsular War: An early 19th-century conflict on the Iberian Peninsula between France, led by Napoleon, and an alliance of Britain, Spain, and Portugal.

perspective: Mathematical laws that allow artists to give the illusion of height, width, depth, and position on a flat surface.

pigment: Colors used in paint from natural sources such as ground-up rocks, metal, and even insects.

portrait: A painting, drawing, or photograph of a person.

Post-Impressionism: A late 19th- and early 20th-century art movement that moved away from the Impressionists' naturalistic use of color and shape.

Renaissance: A time when European artists, writers, and scientists began to think about the world in new ways at the same time as rediscovering the art and learning of the Romans and the Greeks. It lasted several centuries (13th to 16th) and happened at different times in different countries.

Rococo: An elaborate style of art and architecture of the late 18th century. Sometimes called Late Baroque.

Romantic: Describes a painting style dominant in the early 19th century that looked to ancient myths and the natural world for its subject matter.

Royal Academy: The Royal Academy of Arts is an art institution in London set up in the 18th century by artists to encourage and exhibit art.

Russian Revolution: The violent people's rebellions of 1917 in Russia that removed the Russian royal family from power and established a Communist regime.

sculptor: An artist who makes art in three dimensions, often by carving wood, metal, or stone.

self-portrait: A drawing, painting, or photograph of yourself.

still life: A piece of art depicting things that do not move.

Stone Age: A prehistoric period when people used stone to make tools and weapons. It ended about 4,000 years ago.

street art: Art made on the street or in other public places.

studio: The room where an artist works.

Surrealism: A mid 20th-century movement in art and literature that explored the world of dreams and fantasy.

Trafalgar, Battle of: An important sea battle of 1805 when the British Navy defeated the combined naval forces of France and Spain.

Vatican: The tiny city-state located inside Rome that is home to the Pope, head of the Catholic Church.

Western Art: The art that developed from the artistic traditions of Western Europe.

World War II: The world war of 1939 to 1945. It was fought between Germany, Italy, and Japan on the one side against Allied forces on the other that included Britain, Canada, Australia, New Zealand, India, the USA, and many other countries. The Allied forces won.

Index

In memory of Jonathan Hair,
a friend and colleague who loved art, design . . . and motorbikes
Mick, Brita, Rachel, Pete and Matt

STERLING CHILDREN'S BOOKS
New York

An Imprint of Sterling Publishing Co., Inc.
1166 Avenue of the Americas
New York, NY 10036

First Sterling edition published in 2017.

Originally published in 2017 by The Watts Publishing Group Limited

ISBN 978-1-4549-2702-0

Distributed in Canada by Sterling Publishing
c/o Canadian Manda Group, 664 Annette Street
Toronto, Ontario, Canada M6S 2C8

Manufactured in China

Lot #: 10 9 8 7 6 5 4 3 2 1
06/17

sterlingpublishing.com

Credits: *Editor:* Rachel Cooke
Cover design: Peter Scoulding
Design: Peter Scoulding and Matt Lilly, based on an original concept developed by Jonathan Hair and Mick Manning.
Picture researcher: Diana Morris

Picture credits:

Ashmolean Museum, University of Oxford/CC Wikimedia Commons: 14-15. Courtesy of N. Aujoulat, Ministère de la Culture et de la Communication, France: 4-5. Peter Barritt/Superstock: 21. The British Library Board, London: 38-39. Capella degli Scrovengi, Padua/Superstock: 8-9. Christies Images/Superstock © The Estate of Roy Lichtenstein/DACS, London 2017: 80-81. Iakov Filimonov/Shutterstock: front cover picture frames. The Granger Collection/Topfoto: 6. Scott Griessel/Dreamstime: 7b. Guggenheim Museum, New York/The Art Archive/Rex Shutterstock. © Estate of Marc Chagall/DACS, London 2017: 62-63. © Imperial War Museum, London: 73. Kimbell Museum, Fort Worth/CC Wikimedia Commons: 28-29. Kunsthistorisches Museum, Vienna/CC Wikimedia Commons: 24-25. Liaoning Provincial Museum, Shenyang/COM: 12-13. The Louvre, Paris/Peter Willi/Bridgeman Art Library: 7c. The Louvre, Paris/CC Wikimedia Commons: front cover br, 19. Archives H. Matisse. © Succession H. Matisse/DACS, London, 2017: 61. Metropolitan Museum of Art, New York/Bridgeman Art Library: 55. Museo del Prado, Madrid/Classic Paintings/Alamy: 40-41. Museo del Prado, Madrid/CC Wikimedia Commons: 33. Museum of Modern Art, New York/Bridgeman Art Library. © Salvador Dali, Fundacio Gala-Salvador Dali/DACS, London 2017: 66. Museum of Modern Art, New York/CC Wikimedia Commons: front cover cl, 48-49. National Gallery of Art, Canberra/Bridgeman Art Library. © The Pollock-Krasner Foundation/ARS, NY and DACS, London 2017: 76-77. National Gallery, London/Bridgeman Art Library: 11, 22-23, 46-47, 50-51. The National Gallery, Oslo/Bridgeman Art Library: front cover tr, 52. National Museum, Stockholm (CC BY SA): 57. Private Collection/AKG © The Estate of Frida Kahlo/DACS, London 2017: 74. Private Collection/Bridgeman Art Library. © The Estate of Jean-Michel Basquiat/DACS, London 2017: 83. Private Collection/Bridgeman Art Library. © Estate of Pierre Bonnard/DACS, London 2017: 58-59. Private Collection/Christies. © The Estate of L.S. Lowry/DACS, London 2017: 78-79. Private Collection/Fine Art Images/Superstock. © The Estate of Pablo Picasso/DACS, London 2017: 71. Private Collection/Hans Heinz/Artothek. © The Estate of Tamara de Lempicka/DACS, London 2017: 64. Private Collection/CC Wikimedia Commons: 37. Rijksmuseum, Amsterdam/Alamy: 31. Rijksmuseum, Amsterdam/CC Wikimedia Commons: 35. Tabley House Collection, University of Manchester/Bridgeman Art Library: 42-43. Uffizi Gallery, Florence/CC Wikimedia Commons: 16-17. UIG/Superstock: 27. Whitney Museum of American Art, New York. Gift of Calvin Klein/AKG. © Georgia O'Keeffe Museum/DACS, London 2017: 69. CC Wikimedia Commons: 7t. World History Archive/Alamy: 44-45.

In 1940, Picasso went to see the newly discovered Lascaux cave paintings. He was amazed by what he saw.